the Best Thoughts to Think

to Think

five minutes before

*Harnessing the power of pre-sleep minutes
to help realize your dreams*

Kate Martin
Illustrated by Scott Fricke

BALBOA
PRESS

A DIVISION OF HAY HOUSE

Balboa Press books may be ordered through booksellers or by contacting:

Balboa Press
A Division of Hay House
1663 Liberty Drive
Bloomington, IN 47403
www.balboapress.com
1 (877) 407-4847

Because of the dynamic nature of the Internet, any web addresses or links contained in
this book may have changed since publication and may no longer be valid. The views
expressed in this work are solely those of the author and do not necessarily reflect the views
of the publisher, and the publisher hereby disclaims any responsibility for them.

The author of this book does not dispense medical advice or prescribe the use of any technique
as a form of treatment for physical, emotional, or medical problems without the advice of a
physician, either directly or indirectly. The intent of the author is only to offer information
of a general nature to help you in your quest for emotional and spiritual well-being. In the
event you use any of the information in this book for yourself, which is your constitutional
right, the author and the publisher assume no responsibility for your actions.

Any people depicted in stock imagery provided by Thinkstock are models,
and such images are being used for illustrative purposes only.
Certain stock imagery © Thinkstock.

Cover design by Lizzie Tenant.

Print information available on the last page.

ISBN: 978-1-5043-5744-9 (sc)
ISBN: 978-1-5043-5750-0 (e)

Balboa Press rev. date: 08/17/2016

For

Lizzie

CONTENTS

Look for the top hat after each of the six best thoughts. Here
you will find a ready-reference to help you practice the technique
introduced in the chapter.

Suggestions for Enjoying This Book

What if you learned that you had the power within to dramatically change your life for the better simply by altering one daily five-minute activity? No push-ups required. No need to cut out sweets or change your spending habits, although this could lead to any or all of these if you so desire. Would you be interested in learning more? If so, consider this your handbook.

Through the use of six techniques based on the research of both scientists and psychologists, you will discover the ways in which *pre-sleep thoughts* influence the direction of your life. You will be introduced to the amazing, hardworking conscious mind as well as the ever vigilant and abiding unconscious mind who work together to help create your world. Armed with this knowledge, you will discover your ability to bring your heart's desires straight to you.

The message of this book is intended to appeal to the child in all of us and therefore is provided with illustrations and written with an uplifting rhyme scheme. It beckons the one who was filled with wonder and awe, the one who made seeking fun a priority, and most importantly, the one who focused on capacity and was in the habit of saying, "Look what I can do!" because *this* person never doubted and always recognized their magnificent and unique self!

While the style of writing lends a light-hearted tone to the book, it may take some rereading to best comprehend the message. Better yet, read it aloud, or have someone read to you, or … read aloud *with* someone!

However you choose to use it
is in your hands, kid.
Be steady and stick with it.
You'll be happy you did!

THE SETTING

The Prime Time to Change Your Mind

Late at night, oh so sleepy,
so drowsy,
dozing off in bed,
one sheep, two sheep, three sheep, four …
                what wretched worries ambush your head!

They come from behind,
they come from within,
all around and unbidden,
they worm their way in.

They are the *can'ts* and the *won'ts*
and those *nasty-never-wills*,
the *shouldn't-haves* and
the *might-have beens.*

But for now, just be still!

Such worrisome wailings
are *not* good at all
and the power they pack
before sleep is *not* small.

Although it's no secret, very few
people know that our
thoughts before sleep
set the stage for a show.
It's a show that's performed
based on thoughts that *you've* thought
and directed by feelings that every thought brought.

And of all the brain's business
conducted in a day, those brief thoughts,
pre-sleep, steal the show in your play.

"Now hold up a minute!"
You shake your head as you wince.
"This is clear as dishwater, and I'm not yet convinced!"

Well, in this book are techniques, "Best Thoughts" if you will, to help *you*
quell your worries and to do so with skill.

Through pictures and rhyme,
these pages explain it,
making it easy for all to retain it.

So sit back or lie down,
and enjoy what you read.
Right now, before sleep,
this is just what you need.

You're sleepy,
you're blinking,
you're starting to snore.
Here are …

the best thoughts
to think
five minutes before.

THE CAST & CREW

Introducing You to the Powers Within

That cumbrous boulder that sits on the shoulders,
to keep raised on some days —a burden.
Never balk at the load, for inside its hold
lies the most precious cargo, for certain.

Yes, let's respect that rock of a noggin—
for it cradles the dear Conscious Mind.
You know *him* well; *he's* the one you tell
to think what you think
all the time.

Conscious:

the prolific performer,
entrusted to meet your vast quota
of over eighty thousand thoughts per day;

he's a bit of a brain showboat-a!

No kidding! Each day, we do it (and so the experts deem).
I'll say it again: eighty thousand … plus ten—

the Conscious is one busy bean!

He does all your learning,

                    he remembers your past,

        he helps you make choices

                  and plans that will last.

Yes, while you are awake,

               he's your prime contemplator,

               a deputy of daydream,

               your noodle's narrator.

But ... he's not a solo artist!

No, your program would not be complete
were it not
for the *finesse* of the artist *noblesse*
you're about to meet.

Let's draw back the curtain,
meet the chap with the flair,
the genius behind ... all your designs,
the "Artisan Extraordinaire!"

The *one* and the *only,*
at your service all the time—
backstage,
designing,
you'll find ...

the grand
Unconscious Mind!

Yes, the Unconscious Mind
is responsible for
your *show's* production—

                    but also much, much more!

A masterful designer,
a "Johnny on the Spot"
gathering props to match your thoughts
(whether the thoughts are true or not).

Your unconscious concierge is there to support
whatever you think and *all*
you purport.
To correct what you think, well,
that just won't compute!

             From the Unconscious Mind, you'll get no dispute!

He's not the best friend
who says, "*Noooo*, that's not true!"
when you feel compelled to talk badly—of you.

So, if you think,

Gee, I'm stupid,

your Unconscious says,

"You bet!
Why, you're the stupidest person I've ever met!"

Then he runs behind the stage,
scouring all around
to find
props to help prove
your presumption profound!

Using pictures and memories, your designer will go far
to take your little "I am stupid"

and stage a great big
"Yes, you are!"

So go ahead … tell yourself,
"I am ugly,"
"I am shy,"
"I am scared,"
"I am broke."
Say it, because you will be. Know why?

Because *you* turned your fear right into belief,
setting Unconscious to work for eight hours of sleep!

"Stage left and stage right,
people. Get to your mark!
No time to slack off—
we have a show here to start!"

"Turn down the lights,
for this scene must be dismal!
Fetch me that soundtrack
that makes one feel miserable!"

"Let's open with 'You're Stupid!'
follow up with 'Nobody Cares,'
a quick comedy skit, 'You Lazy Half-Wit,'
then bring the house down with 'Life Isn't Fair!'"

And when you wake up,
Oh, the show can continue, behavior you've directed
to be selected within you.
So, if you feel inadequate,
it's time you understand
that you direct the show of life
with the help of a great stagehand.

But old habits can change.
It's so easy to do:
retrain your brain to
stage a new show for you!

Don't worry now or bother; "best thoughts" are reliable,
and your brain is neuroplastic! What?
(It means that it's pliable!)

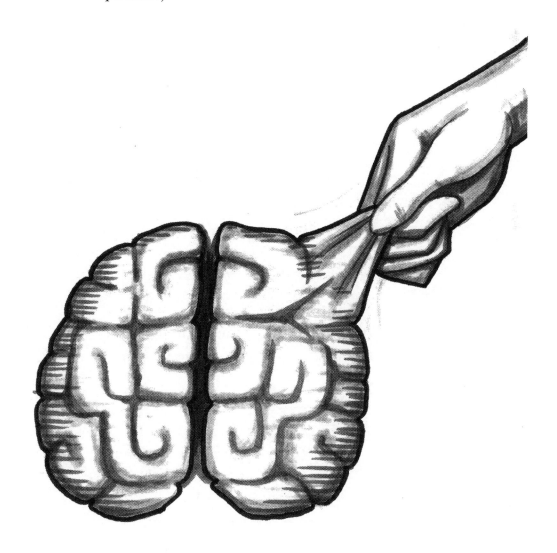

And never forget:
you can train yourself to best use your mind
to bring wishes fulfilled of the ultimate kind.

Here is the secret to
retraining your head:
Start the process at night
before *you* go to bed!

The chapters that follow bring suggestions, light-hearted,
and the direction you'll need to get re-training started.

BEST THOUGHT NO. 1

—Scratching the Old Script—

The premiere of your new production
is just around the bend,
but before you bring in new acts,
the bad acts need to end!

This task may seem daunting,
but I assure you it's not so,
for those that frown on you
are the first acts that must go:

There's an act based on guilt,
there's one built on blame,
a relentless routine
of self-judgment and shame.

Let's scratch these acts,
these long-repeating,
self-defeating,
raucous rants of
bogus bleating!

Yes, indeed, these are lousy,
but do you favor one worse,
performed for so long
you need never rehearse?

It's the late-night show special
in which you engage
the "I Don't Have Enough!" show
each night, center stage.

I don't have enough money.
I don't have enough skill.
I don't have enough time, talent, or will

to do that thing that I desire
or get the things that I want.
I don't have what's required;
my supply is simply … scant!

Why, there are *lots* of enoughs;
tons of bundles abound.
There are infinite enoughs for all,
plenty of enoughs to go around!

So, what is it that's blocking
your endless supply?
Is it *you* and your thoughts
made of *doubts* that deny?

Let's start by setting these thoughts aside.
    Let's see what happens when
you learn a trick to stop them quick.
    Let's see what happens then.

If you want to learn how
to keep bad thoughts at bay,
just say what I say,
and then do what I say,

Are you ready to learn?
Do you want to know how?
Just say,
"Thanks," to the thoughts;
then add, "Not now!"

Yes, be sure to say, "Thanks."
There's no need to be gruff.
But be firm when you say,
"Not now, that's enough!"

Put your hand on your shoulder, and then, as you say,
"Thanks, but not now," you will brush them away.

When the pesky thoughts ask,
"But how? But why? But when?"
repeat the same words over again:
"Thanks, but not now.
Thanks, but not now."

These four words are potent,
psychologically legit,
so deliver with trust
for the most benefit.

It is as though you are setting
a reserved sign in place:
*Only VIP thoughts
are allowed in this space!*

Do this each night,
five minutes before.

Start right away.
Then go on to learn more!

Thanks, but not now!

Thanks, but not now!

Thanks, but not now!

BEST THOUGHT NO. 2

—Upstaging the Illusions—

Do you have faith?
Do you have a bit of trust?
Do you believe in something?
Or do you ask, "Like what?"

You have a choice before you,
a simple one to hear:
you can
choose to place your faith in love or
place your faith in fear.

Most of those around you unknowingly
made a choice.
They will tell you there is much to fear, and
bark with a bothersome voice.

They blare on the news!

        They blast in the street!

                They bellow the blues!

So many you meet—
            have more faith in what they fear
                could "grave" us
            than they have in the power of love
                to save us.

And now,
five minutes before,
as you create your show,
a bit
about the science of fear that
you'd do well to know:

Fear is all-consuming!
It renders conscious inept as
            adrenaline flows
                to all the brain lobes,
alerting each one of a threat.

            When adrenaline pumps up,
                your intelligence deflates,
            for muscle takes rank when your life is at stake!

So,
imagine you're on safari
when a tiger comes in sight.
Your mind will reject your intellect
and instinctively flee or fight.

This is a good thing!
(Nobody could knock it.)
It's a swell trait to store in the instinctual pocket.

But ... when imminent danger is absent,
do you fire-up false states of fear
by *dwelling* on dark imaginings
you've convinced yourself will appear?

Your body can't handle lots and lots.
It can do fear in spurts.
It can do fear in spots!
Worry and bother leave judgement impaired
'cause you can't do smart things
when you're doing things ... scared!

So, giddy up, you danger rangers—

those who've mastered defaulting to fright,
obsessed with questions, projections of woe,
with your list of what-ifs near at night.

What if *this* happens?
What if *they* won't?
What if *it* doesn't?
What if *I* don't?

Say, "Thanks, but not now."
Then
jump to it, and
fill the gap in
with any pleasing options
that you suppose can happen!

Let go of the what-ifs
that go after catastrophe.
Five minutes before, try,
"I can't wait to see ..."

I can't wait to see ...
I'm excited to know ...
I can't wait to find out
what turns up in my show!

These lines are compelling; you must trust and accede,
for unconscious and
its Source
will bring forth *everything* you need.

Fear is our *biggest* problem,
our hitch, our *original* sin.
When you trust and exchange your fear for love,
your purpose-filled life can begin.

This is trick #2,
the key to joy's door;
choose love over fear

five minutes before.

Tonight's Thoughts of Love and Trust
to replace the "What-ifs."

I can't wait to see …
I wonder what will show up …
I am so excited to find out …
I don't know how it can happen,
but I can't wait to learn …
I trust that good things are already on their way!
I'm joyful to know that, with love,
all things good are possible!

BEST THOUGHT NO. 3

—Sacred Soliloquy—

"Lights … camera … STOP the ACTION!"
Unconscious flags the crew—
"Why, this bloke just broke up blabber
I've grown most accustomed to!"

"Quiet on the set,
for I sense something new."
Unconscious now fixated as he waits
for his next cue.

"But where to from here?
What now?" Conscious yells.
"With problems *on hold,*
on what shall I dwell?"

Say it: "Thanks, but not now!"

There's no need for stage fright!

Then read on, and enjoy
this next thought for tonight …

Did you know that *you* have a
power existing,
smack-dab center heart that you
might be resisting?
Well, are you a member of the human club?
(Of course you are, so that's rhetorical.)
Then you've been forged with a superpower,
nothing less than

phantasmagorical!

It was packed in your box
on the day you were shipped!
It came with directions!
It came with your script!

But … sometimes *it* happens …

The power gets lost,
buried beneath
or unwittingly tossed
when a
young heart
gets bruised

or broken
or busted

      by someone who's loved,
      by someone who's trusted.

But it's the ticket to your *greatest show*!
Now's the time that you *reclaim it*!
It is well within your reach now—
grab it, feel it, and exclaim it!

"I *am* and I *can*!
I *am* and I *can*!"
At night before sleep,
again and *again*—

This is it!
It's the ticket to take with you to bed!
Forget the "I can'ts," and say, "I *can*," instead!

(How is it that one, as noble as you,
allows "can't" to jump out
before "am" and "can do"?)

And ... when you say "can't," might you be denying
the Source of the love on whom you're relying?

If you're one to spout,
"No, I can't ... no, not me!"
take a leap, have some faith
in yourself,
and you'll see
the magnificent power *you've* been given to share.
Retrieve it, embrace it, and believe that it's there!

The Unconscious will revel in the new words you send it, yelling,
"Strike that old set, for our run here has ended!"

Say, "I *am*, and I *can*!"
with *belief* and with *trust*.
Right before sleep, this thought is a must.
Yes, this trick #3
is so easy to do, but
can something so simple bring dreams straight to you?

Yes, it can, and it will,
and yet few people do it.

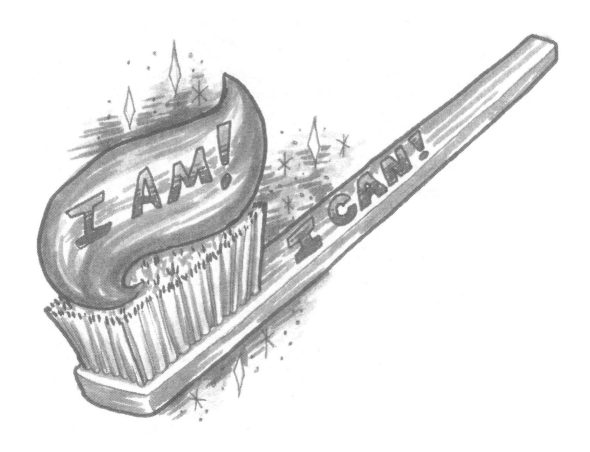

But *you* know the secret,
so brush your teeth,
and get to it!

Say it slowly.

Say it loudly.

Say it softly.

Say it proudly.

And … to serve as a reminder, find a dry-erase and write
these key words on your mirror—

Flash that smile
as you recite!

I am, and I can!

I am, and I can!

I am, and I can!

BEST THOUGHT NO. 4

—An Evening Monologue—

Now, let's use this momentum to amend
what you say
about *you*,
to yourself,
at the end of the day.

It's time to repeat affirmations
or pick a mantra to serve
you and your desires.
(Yes, a phrase or a word
that describes who you are
at the core of your spirit,
and generates emotion
every time that you hear it.)

Some folks might argue,
"How boastful of you!
You must focus on your faults, 'cause … er … well,
that's just what *we* do."

Yep, and I'll bet you a gumball
the same folks have a flurry
of mantras made up
all day long based on worry!

Like the cant's, the wont's,
and nasty-never-wills,
They recite them with ease.
They spew them with skill.
"I don't have enough,
and I want to have more.
I'm so low on money.
Guess I'll always be poor!"

"I never have time to do
things that are fun.
I am way, way too busy
getting all my work done."

"I just don't fit in,
and I'm always so bored.
Others seem to find friends,
but I'm always ignored."

"Oh, she looks so lovely.
I can't look like that.
I've got my mom's nose.
Besides … I'm too fat!"

"With my rotten luck, why should I try it?
You can *tell* me I can,
but I really don't buy it."

Okay, that's enough!
How ill are you feeling?
These sickening scripts
send one's stomach to reeling!

Affirmations?
You got it!
We chant them all day
in our mind and out loud, but what kind do *you* say?

We all pick "head scripts," but
take guard of the kind
that honor self-doubt
staking claim in your mind.

Now here is a challenge,
a little chore to get done.
Tomorrow you'll count them ... each and every one!
Use a hatch mark to tally every troubling thing you think.

You'll be amazed when you learn
how many things you think stink.

Bad thoughts are a habit,
a bad habit of gab.
Drab blabber running rabid—
better nab it while you can!

Besides …
it's not truthful,
since you
are divine,
to describe yourself anything
less than sublime.

Children don't *see* faults;
they seek out capacity.
They *will find* it and *remind* you,

"I can do it! Look at me!"

So, get busy tonight
with your new state of mind,

proclaiming the positive, out loud, at bedtime!

And how about this?
There's a list to peruse
of new
lines to rehearse
to be kept where you snooze.
Pick three, five, or ten
that speak to your heart.
Then recite them; believe them
                    in bed when it's dark.

The grand designer within
will grab them and dash,
yelling,

               "To the prop box, young ward.
                 We must move in a flash!

                 We've only eight hours
                 at most, Conscious Page,
                 to rewrite tomorrow,
                 to reset the stage!"

Ahem …

Don't forget this is science;

there's a brain scan that shows

when we think *happy* thoughts—

                    Our gray matter glows.

So where is this list?

On the next page it's shown,

but come in closer, pssst …

                    you can also make up your own.

I am.

I am love.

I am divine.

I am brilliant.

I am strong.

I am prosperous.

I am intentional.

I am creative.

I am a healer.

I am beautiful.

I am healthy.

I am energetic.

I am joyful.

I am thankful.

I am worry- and problem-free.

I am able to find beauty everywhere.

I am in control of my thoughts.

I am able to attract good things.

I am living in abundance.

I am created to succeed.

I am filled with trust and faith.

I am growing in every way.

I am always connected with my Source.

I can.

I can love.

I can create.

I can heal.

I can relax.

I can trust.

I can forgive.

I can laugh often.

I can create my world.

I can bring peace and light.

I can fulfill my heart's desires.

I can share my gifts with others.

I can find answers with ease.

I can see innocence in others.

I can dismiss fearful thoughts.

I can believe in love.

I can see beauty.

I can attract good things.

I can love living.

I can live, loving.

Now own your own.

Write them in red.
Recite them in bed!
Whatever it takes,
get them into your head!

I am …   I can …
I am …   I can …
I am …   I can …
I am …   I can …
I am …   I can …
I am …   I can …
I am …   I can …
I am …   I can …
I am …   I can …

BEST THOUGHT NO. 5

—A Little Ad-Libbing—

Now you are ready
to create lofty notions,
to think higher thoughts
that stir joyful emotions.

What?

Okay, it's time to design
a scene that is real.

Imagine, and *be in it*,
until the point that you *feel*,
exactly as you would if your
imagined dream was true.

Emotion is the magnet

that attracts these things to you.

Heaven knows we feel yucky
when we dwell on dismal things—
Time to bask in the light that bright thinking brings.

Caution: Stay away from the *will-bes, will-dos,* and *somedays.*
Imagine it's true *now, today,* and *always.*

Do you know what to do?
Are the directions all clear?
It's time to *create,*
right now, right here!

Five minutes each night,
design your own dreams.
You can *see, hear, touch (smell?)*
all you choose for each scene.

Scene 1
Instead of walking today,
You've decided to fly.
Look around— holy cow!—
a duck just flew by.

Scene 2
Your name was just called—
an award winning occasion.
The crowd jumps to their feet.
It's your standing ovation!

Scene 3
You're swimming through deep grass,
jetting like an otter—
rolling, gliding freely,
you're at home now
under water.

Scene 4
Oh, the sand feels so warm
as you lie on this beach,
soaking up the sun now,
with surfboard in reach.

This is thought #5!
Do you know what to do?
Your wish is fulfilled.
Now *feel* that it's true!

Oh, it can't be over stated:
feeling is the trigger
for Unconscious to deliver
dreams more quickly and lots bigger.

The sky has no limit;
common sense can't confine you!
Go ahead, dip your toes
in a pool of "anything goes,"
where awesome and astounding define you!

Do this each night,
and over time you will see
life shifting and flowing
rather synchronistically.

Good fortune will sit next to the

break you've waited for.

Dreams and wishes so mysteriously

come knocking at your door.

Now you won't fail to notice.
No!
You'll spot them right away. Embrace them,
then escort them to the place they're meant to stay.

But … remember what happens; I'm sorry to repeat it.
If you say, "I can't have it," your Unconscious believes it.

Say,
"Yes, I am worthy!
Yes, I can do!
Yes, I can see
my dreams have come true!"

And now it's *your* turn!
Have fun and design
from the limitless Source
of dreams in your mind.

In the event Conscious panics at night
before bed,

spouting,
"I haven't *one* dream
to pull from the head!"

Relax, ya little wart!
You can make a dream display,
a teleprompter of sorts,
to get you on your way.

You can draw, you can paint,
to create your dream scenes,
or scrounge around till you've found
some old magazines.

Page through and find any
pictures that seem
to visually capture a
wish or a dream.
Go ahead! Cut them out!
Use tape or get glue,
and paste up a patchwork
of passions beaucoup!

(And don't forget the Internet; there are
plenty of pictures online you can get.)

To give it more power, add
finesse and add flavor.
Paste tasty words
for Unconscious to savor.

Add

    abundance.

Add

    trust.

Add

    love in bold letters.

Add

    I *am*
    and I *can.*

Add

    your name as a header.

Before sleep, keep it handy;
it will serve as a spark
to ignite the best scenes
        in your thoughts
                in the dark.

And, as you gaze at a picture,
don't wish, want, or crave it.
Think thoughts of *having*,
        feel it, and then *save* it.

This teleprompter,
        this guy in the wings, will help
find your bearings
when you lose such things.

Play the part tonight,
        and believe your wishes true.
        With practice, practice, practice,
        you'll attract good things to you!

MY DREAM-STORMING PAGE
(Jot down ideas for your dream-display as they come to you.)

BEST THOUGHT NO. 6

—A Dialogue of Gratitude—

"Ought to," "should have,"
"could have," "would have,"
"might have," "can't have"—
whoa!

Do you need to be reminded that they love to steal the show?

Yes, your ego would suggest it's best
to fret before you rest
for ego *is* self-doubt.
It *is* guilt and it's *regret*.

Let's change the view!
Let's dump regret!
(You know it never served you yet.)

Your program has an opening
in which you can devote
five minutes of contemplation to
a simple thank-you note.

Who will you thank
for what they have done?
Who made good choices?

You—you're the one!

Little things,
big things,
easy things
bringing light,

healthy things,
kind things make
fun thoughts
tonight.

Time for practice!

(Say your name here) Thanks for getting up on time, when you really wanted to snooze.
(You) Thanks for giving that thing away that you really wanted to use.
(You) Thanks for helping him with that even though it made you late.
(You) Thanks for letting her step in line, knowing you would have to wait.
(You) Thanks for choosing water, when you might have had a pop.
(You) Thanks for knowing when words got harsh; you knew that you should stop.

You picked that up. You smiled at them.
    You let it go. You tried again.
You said you were sorry. You washed off the table.

Before biting that bar, you read the food label.
You gave a hug. You shared your lunch.

You petted that dog. Thanks a bunch!

What a day you have had!
How much good you have done!
How much better the world
because you have come!

This trick is a favorite
'cause it brings such surprise
when you
go through your day
and at once realize the number and kind
of good things you do,
and how pleasing it is to say thank you to *you*!

And if you choose to dwell on just
one deed of good,
well, it will serve *ten times* more than
one hundred woes would.

Yes, we all have our snags, but
in here lies the rub;
when we focus on faults …

                our goodness gets snubbed.

        Yes, we're cemented with intent to love,
           and it's best to be inclined
        to set your sights on such each night—-

Seek and you shall find.

You're *no random egg*.

You're a *high-bred* who hatched,

created with *craft*,

then divinely dispatched

to do what you do

with ease every day.

Take notice, *good egg*,

tout de suite.

Don't delay!

My Thank You Notes ...

Thanks for _____

Thanks for _____

Thanks for _____

Thanks for _____

Thanks for _____

Thanks for _____

Thanks for _____

Thanks for _____

Thanks for _____

Thanks for _____

Thanks for _____

Thanks for _____

Thanks for _____

Thanks for _____

Thanks for _____

How about some verbs
to help keep you on track
while you focus on good
each night, looking back …

Thanks for:
doing …
showing …
helping …
knowing …
encouraging …
listening …
sharing …
assisting …
smiling …
guiding …
hugging …
providing …
stopping …
telling …
trying …
not yelling …
laughing …
empathizing …
hearing …
realizing …

TAKE ONE ... TAKE TWO

Allowing Change to Come in Good Time

You've probably heard it
and no doubt know it's true.

> For long-term results, quick fixes won't do.

You've got to stick with it!
> A few tries won't suffice.

(Will your biceps be buff
> if you exercise ... twice?)

No!

So pick a thought from this book.
Pick two, or pick three
every night before sleep
for three weeks, and you'll see.
After time passes,
take a quick glance behind;
you may be surprised
by the changes you find.

And one last little hint, and please bend your ear near!

Use the tricks in this book
with *ease* and good *cheer.*

Don't try so hard.
Don't strive and strain.

Step into your heart
as you retrain your brain!

It can happen to you,
and you may just be shocked
when you find all the doors
your "best thoughts" have unlocked.

Now *you* have the power
to reboot your thinking
five minutes before
when you're yawning
and blinking.

YOUR NEW REPERTOIRE

Realizing Your *New* Show!

The audience is gathering.
    Backstage, the crew is set.
        The guy in the wings is ready to bring
            prompts so you won't forget.

"Thanks but not now!" to any
thoughts based on fear.
    The stage is yours now,
    and they
    don't belong here!

With bad acts removed,
you can *now* show your stuff
as you project and deliver,
"I do have enough!"

Because
"I *am*, and I *can*"
is the *truth*—there's no doubt!

Time to trade in "what-ifs" for

"My show *will* turn out!"

Mantras on the catwalk.
Affirmations in the aisle.
Lofty notions in the green room.
Bring your best *thoughts*—
Flash that smile!

And remember …
        that chum behind the curtain

stands ready at the rig.

Be diligent as you direct;

play small no more.

Play big!

But wait, there's a bit more …

A list of books,
a list of songs,
sleep-inducing aromas and foods,
a variety of helpful hints,
and each has been pre-chewed!

Of course,
That's just a figure of speech.
It's nice to have resources at night within reach.

So, a sampling of tidbits
have been "tasted" for you;
you'll find them up next,
under "Good Sleep Menu."

Good Sleep Menu

Select from a variety of musical appetizers per your personal taste:

Pop/Rock Music

Elizaveta "Dreamer"

Peter Gabriel "Down to Earth"

The Beatles "Tell Me What You See"

Cider Sky "Glowing in the Dark" and "Shooting Stars"

Coldplay "Paradise" and "Strawberry Swing"

Alyssa Bonagura "I Make My Own Sunshine"

Stacy Clark "Anywhere"

Jason Mraz "Living in the Moment"

Electronic and New Age Music

Marconi Union "Weightless"

Electra "Airstream"

Cafe Del Mar "We Can Fly"

Cusco "Da Gama" and "Tigris & Euphrates"

Baraka "Berceuse"

Steven Halpern "Relaxation Suite I"

Jim Brickman "Beautiful," "Timeless," and "Blessings"

Classical Music

Philip Glass "The Complete Piano Etudes"

David Lanz "Return to the Heart"

Pachelbel with Ocean "Live and Let Live"

Robin Spielberg "Dreaming of Summer"

For the hearty appetite, enjoy a taste of these
spirit-lifting literature selections:

Wayne Dyer
There's a Spiritual Solution to Every Problem
The Power of Intention
Wishes Fulfilled

Marianne Williamson
A Return to Love
Illuminata

Julia Cameron
The Artist's Way
Walking in This World: The Practical Art of Creativity

Dana Wilde
Train Your Brain: How to Build a Million Dollar Business in Record Time

Tama Kieves
Inspired & Unstoppable: Wildly Succeeding in Your Life's Work!
This Time I Dance!

Don Miguel Ruiz
The Voice of Knowledge
The Mastery of Love

Lisa Nichols
No Matter What!: 9 Steps to Living the Life You Love

Richard Nelson Bolles

What Color Is Your Parachute?

Mike Dooley

Infinite Possibilities: The Art of Living Your Dreams

Here are some selections on the lighter side of literature:

Max Lucado
You Are Special
You Are Mine

Tama Kieves
A Year Without Fear: 5-minute mind-set shifts

Dan Zadra
5: Where Will You Be Five Years from Today?

*Top it all off with any of these delightful sleep-promoting treats found **on-line**:*

David L. Katz, MD: *Foods to Help You Sleep Better*

Joy Bauer: *Eat Your Way to a Good Night's Sleep*

Jim Long: *Making Herbal Dream Pillows: Secret Blends for Pleasant Dreams (The Spirit of Aromatherapy)*

Cathy Wong: *Sleep Aids: 14 Natural Remedies to Get a Better Night's Rest*

Pre-Sleep Resources: My Personal Favorites
(Keep a list of additional resources that *you* discover and enjoy.)

NOTES

- The phrase "Wishes Fulfilled," used throughout, comes from a title of a book written by Wayne Dyer, *Wishes Fulfilled: Mastering the Art of Manifesting* (2012).

- In this same book, Wayne Dyer speaks of the dramatic influence of pre-sleep thoughts and the direct relationship between reserving this time for positive thoughts and experiencing a fulfilling life.

- Wayne Dyer shares the following additional information in 'Wayne's Blog,' entitled, "How do You Sleep?"

  "Metaphysical teacher Neville Goddard offers us this description of what takes place while we sleep: Sleep is the door through which the conscious, waking mind passes to be creatively joined to the subconscious. Sleep conceals the creative act while the objective world reveals it. In sleep man impresses the subconscious with his conception of himself."

- When speaking of illusions of fear, the closing stanza on page 27 was inspired by a paragraph in Marianne Williamson's book *The Illuminata* (1994, page 27), which reads:

  "Prayer increases our faith in the power of good and thus our power to invoke it. Most of us have more faith in AIDS to kill us than we have faith in God to heal us and make us whole. We have more faith in the power of violence to destroy us than we have faith in the power of love to restore us. Where we place our faith, there will we find our treasure."

- The initial background information regarding the power of positive thinking and its connection with the unconscious mind was found in Dana Wilde's book, *Train Your Brain.*

- Through my research I learned that the terms *subconscious* and *unconscious* are at times interchangeable. However, by definition, they do indeed refer to two different aspects of our human psyche, and since the former is not a term recognized by the psychlogical community, I chose to follow Dana Wilde's lead and use the word unconscious for the purpose here. This term is used to desribe that part of us which controls our involuntary systems as well as takes direction from the conscious mind in order to shape our identity and our lives.

ACKNOWLEDGEMENTS

I am so thankful for those who supported and inspired me as well as those who contributed in order to bring this project to completion, especially the following:

My daughter, Elizabeth Tenant, for her sharp intellect—keen eyes and ears, her loyalty and compassion, and for her unwavering willingness to stop whatever she was doing to patiently respond to the inquiry "Lizzie, what do you think of *this* line?"

I am grateful for Jim Bemis, my life partner and dear friend. His patience, constant support, and crazy ability to lead silently behind the scenes, allowed this book to unfold.

For Patty Hammes and Liz Modder, for sharing their expansive knowledge of the English language and their kindness with the initial editing process. For Scott Fricke, I am so very pleased he was available to add his delightfully silly slanted talent to this project—A perfect fit!

For being my feedback team and booster club, Liz Kultgen, Nan Martin, Jane Jersild, Joanna Jersild, Peter Martin, Lori Martin, Marilyn Kingore, Jenni Manninen, Gail Katt, and Katie Ballbach. I'm so fortunate to have this gang in my life!

For her grand knowledge as a life coach and for being my constant leg-up person, I am thankful for Reggie Adams— an extraordinary human being! For Dr. Frank Alessi who 'changed my mind' dramatically for the better the day I attended his workshop 15 years ago, and I am grateful that he continues to share his wisdom with me.

I am grateful for the following authors: Wayne Dyer, Marianne Williamson, and Dana Wilde. It is my hope that this book will inspire others to investigate their work. Thank you to all the great staff at Balboa Press. I never imagined I would have access to such a profoundly talented group of professionals.

For mom and dad, who dedicated their lives to the six of us. They were always so delighted with any/all of our accomplishments, so I know their loving spirits are pleased with this book.

Every creative loving effort, no matter how small, changes God's Universe for the better, doesn't it?

Word to My Birds:
• Jordyn • Zac • Luke • Ashley • Caleb • Matt • Noah • Ivan • Lucy • Brian • Francisco • Luciano • Julia • Uriah • Michael • Haley • Luis • Fossen • Brandon • Kaitlyn • Aysia • Braydon • Louie • Levi • Jalah• Andrew • Nichole • Candice • Alex • Sam • Nick • Noah • Dennis • Ernesto • Nakia • Alana • Brittany • Bradley • Daniel • Justin • Michael • Kyle • Jacob • Jessica • David • Autumn • Ted • Jesse • Gustavo • Bryianna • Thomas • Logan • Adrienne • Jeremy • Nolan • Chance • Shaun • Robert • Natalia • Jessica • Tabitha • Eric • Kayla (Schmay)

"You are all uniquely fancy!"

ABOUT THE AUTHOR

Kate Martin has been a high school teacher in Racine, Wisconsin for 27 years working with students with special needs as well as those in general education. She recently retired from teaching to concentrate on training new teachers and parents through her consulting firm, 'The Purposeful Parent.' She also has a degree in vocal performance and sings in various jazz and blues clubs in the area.

Scott Fricke is a native Chicagoan. He studied at The School of the Art Institute of Chicago, and has worked as a professional tattoo artist and an illustrator since 1993.